# Get Well Therapy

W9-BJM-845

# Get Well Therapy

written by
**Clair Bradshaw, R.N.**

illustrated by
R.W. Alley

ONE
CARING
PLACE

Abbey Press

Text © 1996 by Clair Bradshaw
Illustrations © 1996 by St. Meinrad Archabbey
Published by One Caring Place
Abbey Press
St. Meinrad, Indiana  47577

Library of Congress Catalog Number
95-79169


ISBN 0-87029-297-8


Printed in the United States of America

# Foreword

When you're sick, you're sick as a whole person—not just with your physical being but with your mind, your emotions, and your spirit too. Your physical ailment affects every part of you—and, in turn, how every part of you is functioning affects your illness.

So, while you're getting medical advice and care, there's much more you can do to help in your coping and recovery. You can foster a positive attitude, give yourself encouragement, and tap into rich sources of spiritual and psychological strength.

At the same time, you can learn from your illness, and—as unlikely as it may now sound—allow it to enrich your life as it opens your soul to greater wisdom and compassion.

*Get Well Therapy* is a guide to facing illness with your entire being. Its soothing words and illuminating illustrations will encourage and inspire you through the course of recovery, through uncertainty and fear, through loss and change.

Whether you're facing a short-term infirmity, a chronic illness, or a potentially terminal disease, *Get Well Therapy* can help you move toward serenity and peace—and a wellness that transcends the words on a medical chart.

## 1.

Accept the uncertainty of recovery. You cannot know every twist and turn of your journey toward healing. Rest in the only certainty there is— God's embracing love for you.

## 2.

Write down your fears and seal them in an envelope addressed to God. Trust that the Creator has already read what's inside.

## 3.

Choose to be brave. Having courage doesn't mean that you're without fear. It means only that you've decided to act upon life in spite of those fears.

## 4.

Make a commitment to optimism. Though you can't choose your circumstances, you can choose how you respond to them. Having a positive outlook is a choice, not something that just happens to you.

## 5.

Give yourself the time you need to heal. Even if you're usually patient, waiting for recovery can be frustrating. Don't try to race ahead to where you think you should be. Now is the time to listen to your body—like an understanding parent who sets a slower pace to accommodate a child's shorter stride.

# 6.

The healing process is often a mystery, and doctors' prognoses are only predictions based on averages. They don't take into account how unique you are. Remember that you're the expert about your body and what you're able to do.

## 7.

If you think of yourself as a victim of your illness, that's what you'll be. Reach for the role of victor or conqueror instead.

## 8.

Trust your inner voice. Often the Great Healer will speak through your own innate wisdom about your body, emotions, spirit, and will.

## 9.

Set aside a regular meditation time. These moments can become a refuge in a period of crisis, uncertainty, questioning. We often need to be very still to hear God.

# 10.

It's normal to feel sadness and depression when you're not well. Many kinds of losses can come with being sick: changes in your abilities, appearance, job performance, relationships, lifestyle. Face your losses and grieve them. Then you can move on.

## 11.

Anger can be empowering
when it's properly channeled.
Use outrage as an ally in
fighting your infirmity. It
can ward off debilitating
depression and give you the
energy and motivation to get
moving—physically, mentally,
emotionally.

## 12.

The fear of pain and resistance
to it can increase pain
dramatically. Pray for the
strength to lean into the
pain. Explore different pain
management techniques such
as visualization, progressive
relaxation, biofeedback, and
therapeutic massage.

## 13.

Be open to alternative therapies
that honor your soul as well as
your body. Traditional medicine
won't have all the answers
about healing. Your spirit can
be your greatest recovery tool.

## 14.

Sleepless nights can be a special time. Take a warm bath at midnight, indulge in your favorite video at three in the morning, make a list of nice things you can do for yourself, pray for everyone who's in need.

## 15.

Ask for help. You've lent a hand to others in need in the past. There's probably someone in your life who would be genuinely blessed by helping you now.

# 16.

Be loving and bold when asking for assistance. What others think you want may be far from what you really need. You're the expert when it comes to understanding what will help you most.

## 17.

Be thankful for persons who bolster you up; they're a blessing beyond praise. And forgive those who've been unable to support you during recovery. Letting go of your resentment is a gift you give yourself. By dropping the weight of bitterness, you'll ease your journey immeasurably.

## 18.

Redefine what wellness means to you. There may be some things you'll never be able to do again. Work to accept what you can't change. And remember that we're all differently abled.

## 19.

Think of your health changes
as opportunities for new
solutions in your life. The loss
of some abilities may lead you
to discover ones you never knew
you had.

## 20.

If your physical strength is limited in some way, be creative. Occupational and physical therapists, as well as home health nurses, can teach energy-conserving techniques and help you with daily activities.

## 21.

When you feel frustrated about your limitations, be gentle with yourself. Treat yourself as you would a loved one you're nurturing back to health—because that's exactly what you're doing.

## 22.

Let go of any guilt you may feel—for bringing on your illness, for obligations you can't fulfill right now, or simply for not being well. You're responsible for only what you have power over.

## 23.

Recuperation needn't be boring. Use this time for what you never seem to get to: organize a photo album, start a journal, put the kids' schoolwork in a scrapbook, clean out the recipe box.

## 24.

Remember that God is near and suffers with you. As the Great Physician, what God wants most is for your spirit to be restored.

## 25.

You can know peace of mind
and happiness in the midst
of a health crisis. Wellness
encompasses the state of your
spirit as much as the condition
of your body.

## 26.

Try not to think of your illness as punishment. If you're having a hard time remembering that God wants you to be well, a spiritual companion or guide may help you redefine your image of a more loving Creator.

## 27.

Having visitors is a choice, not an obligation. It's not your job to entertain well-wishers. Set your personal boundaries.

## 28.

Be an active partner with your healthcare team. They'll be more effective when they work <u>with</u> you rather than <u>on</u> you.

# 29.

When you're faced with difficult medical decisions, give yourself time to weigh the issues. If possible, write down your thoughts and feelings, seek wise advice, pray over your situation. Then make your own—not anyone else's—decision.

## 30.

Don't let your illness define you. Your identity is so much more. Celebrate all that you are.

## 31.

Consider dialoguing with your illness to find out what it has to tell you. Do you need to change your life direction or to slow down? Is there a crucial ingredient of your inner life that you're neglecting? What can you do to live life more fully?

## 32.

Your response to a major
illness or accident, as with
any other life-changing event,
can strengthen, deepen, and
enrich your character. Search
for evidence of your growth
and celebrate it.

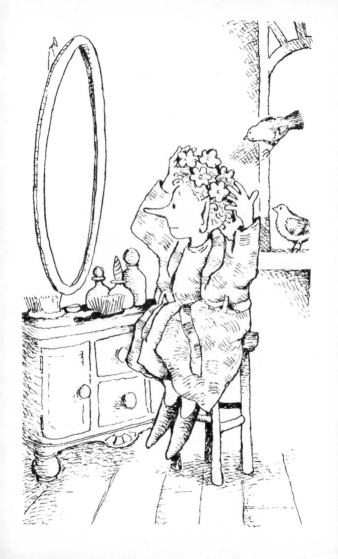

## 33.

Sickness can make you acutely aware of how precious life is. Don't merely weather this crisis; use it to reorder your priorities. Take time to cherish your loved ones and to experience the small joys of everyday life.

## 34.

Deep, abiding compassion for others can arise out of your own suffering. Let your illness open your heart.

## 35.

Make a gratitude list: a cooling breeze, a refreshing glass of lemonade, a cuddling child, more strength today than yesterday, a letter from a friend. Even when everything seems very wrong, search for good things to start that list.

## 36.

It's understandable to be discouraged about slow or no recovery. Let yourself feel your sadness. Share your thoughts with a caring friend. Hold on to the hope that one day these anxious moments will be only a memory.

## 37.

Take heart. When it seems that you'll never get well, ask God's purpose in your suffering. The deepest fulfillment in life comes from surrendering to a Power greater than ourselves. You can find new meaning in life because of this difficult time.

# 38.

Thank God for life.
Each day is a gift.

**Clair Bradshaw** is a registered nurse who has worked with medical and psychiatric patients. "Getting well," she says, "has been a major theme in my life for almost two decades." She has degrees in both nursing and journalism and has written extensively about mental health and spiritual issues. She lives in Bakersfield, California. She is currently working as a home health nurse.

Illustrator for the Abbey Press Elf-help Books, **R.W. Alley** also illustrates and writes children's books. He lives in Barrington, Rhode Island, with his wife, daughter, and son.

# The Story of the Abbey Press Elves

The engaging figures that populate the Abbey Press "elf-help" line of publications and products first appeared in 1987 on the pages of a small self-help book called *Be-good-to-yourself Therapy*. Shaped by the publishing staff's vision and defined in R.W. Alley's inventive illustrations, they lived out author Cherry Hartman's gentle, self-nurturing advice with charm, poignancy, and humor.

Reader response was so enthusiastic that more Elf-help Books were soon under way, a still-growing series that has inspired a line of related gift products.

The especially endearing character featured in the early books—sporting a cap with a mood-changing candle in its peak—has since been joined by a spirited female elf with flowers in her hair.

These two exuberant, sensitive, resourceful, kindhearted, lovable sprites, along with their lively elfin community, reveal what's truly important as they offer messages of joy and wonder, playfulness and co-creation, wholeness and serenity, the miracle of life and the mystery of God's love.

With wisdom and whimsy, these little creatures with long noses demonstrate the elf-help way to a rich and fulfilling life.

**Elf-help Books...adding "a little character" and a lot of help to self-help reading!**

**Get Well Therapy** (perfect-bound)
#20157-4     $4.95     ISBN 0-87029-297-8

**Making-sense-out-of-suffering Therapy**
(perfect-bound)
#20156-6     $4.95     ISBN 0-87029-296-X

**Anger Therapy** (perfect-bound)
#20127-7     $4.95     ISBN 0-87029-292-7

**Caregiver Therapy** (perfect-bound)
#20164-0     $4.95     ISBN 0-87029-285-4

**Self-esteem Therapy** (perfect-bound)
#20165-7     $4.95     ISBN 0-87029-280-3

**Take-charge-of-your-life Therapy** (perfect-bound)
#20168-1     $4.95     ISBN 0-87029-271-4

**Work Therapy** (perfect-bound)
#20166-5     $4.95     ISBN 0-87029-276-5

**Everyday-courage Therapy**
#20167-3     $3.95     ISBN 0-87029-274-9

**Peace Therapy**
#20176-4     $3.95     ISBN 0-87029-273-0

**Friendship Therapy** (perfect-bound)
#20174-9     $4.95     ISBN 0-87029-270-6

**Christmas Therapy** (color edition)
#20175-6     $5.95     ISBN 0-87029-268-4

**Grief Therapy** (perfect-bound)
#20178-0     $4.95     ISBN 0-87029-267-6

**More Be-good-to-yourself Therapy**
#20180-6     $3.95     ISBN 0-87029-262-5

**Happy Birthday Therapy** (perfect-bound)
#20181-4     $4.95     ISBN 0-87029-260-9

**Forgiveness Therapy** (perfect-bound)
#20184-8     $4.95     ISBN 0-87029-258-7

**Keep-life-simple Therapy** (perfect-bound)
#20185-5     $4.95     ISBN 0-87029-257-9

**Be-good-to-your-body Therapy** (perfect-bound)
#20188-9     $4.95     ISBN 0-87029-255-2

**Celebrate-your-womanhood Therapy** (perfect-bound)
#20189-7     $4.95     ISBN 0-87029-254-4

**Acceptance Therapy** (color edition)
#20182-2     $5.95     ISBN 0-87029-259-5

**Acceptance Therapy** (regular edition)
#20190-5     $3.95     ISBN 0-87029-245-5

**Keeping-up-your-spirits Therapy** (perfect-bound)
#20195-4     $4.95     ISBN 0-87029-242-0

**Play Therapy** (perfect-bound)
#20200-2     $4.95     ISBN 0-87029-233-1

**Slow-down Therapy** (perfect-bound)
#20203-6     $4.95     ISBN 0-87029-229-3

**One-day-at-a-time Therapy**
#20204-4     $3.95     ISBN 0-87029-228-5

**Prayer Therapy** (perfect-bound)
#20206-9     $4.95     ISBN 0-87029-225-0

**Be-good-to-your-marriage Therapy** (perfect-bound)
#20205-1     $4.95     ISBN 0-87029-224-2

**Be-good-to-yourself Therapy** (hardcover)
#20196-2     $10.95     ISBN 0-87029-243-9

**Be-good-to-yourself Therapy** (perfect-bound)
#20255-6     $4.95     ISBN 0-87029-209-9

Available at your favorite bookstore or directly from us at
One Caring Place, Abbey Press Publications,
St. Meinrad, IN 47577. Or call 1-800-325-2511.